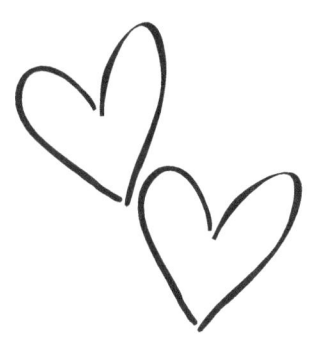

This book belongs to:

_____

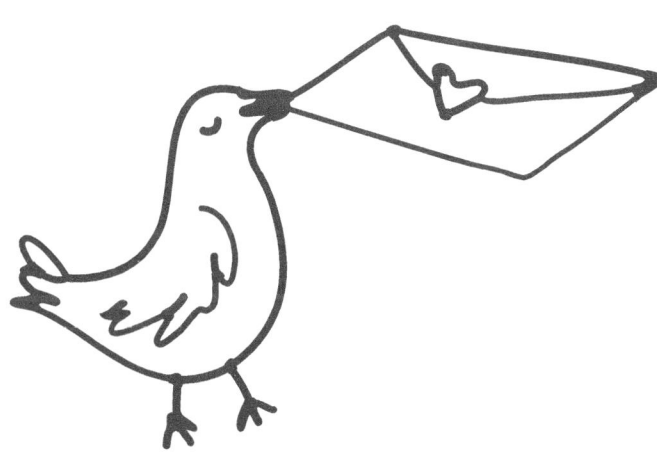

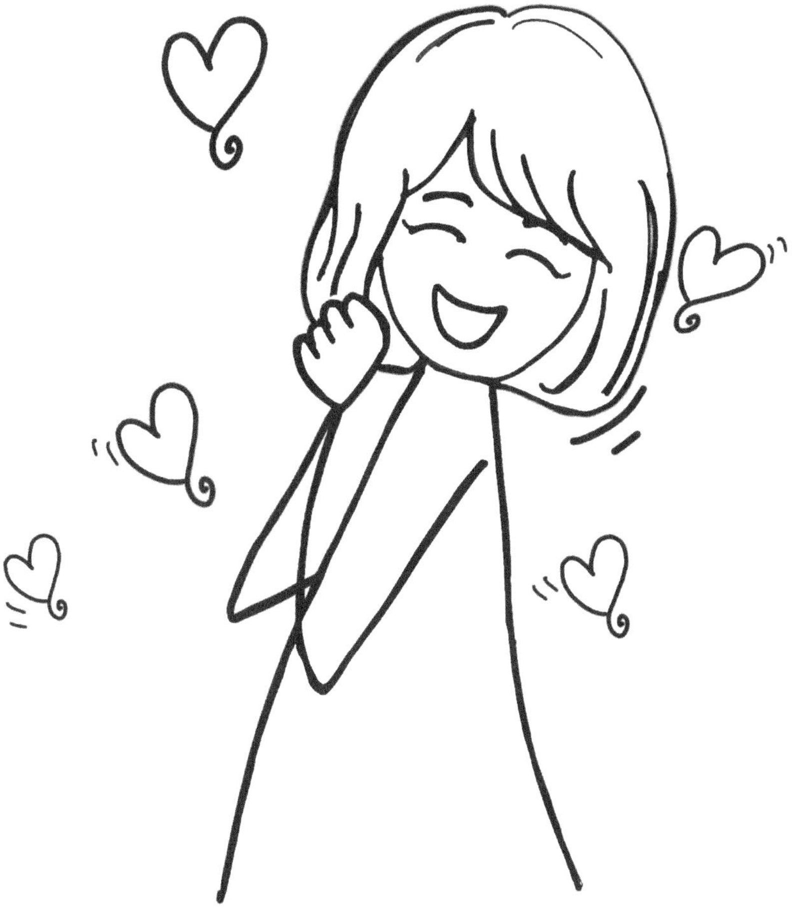

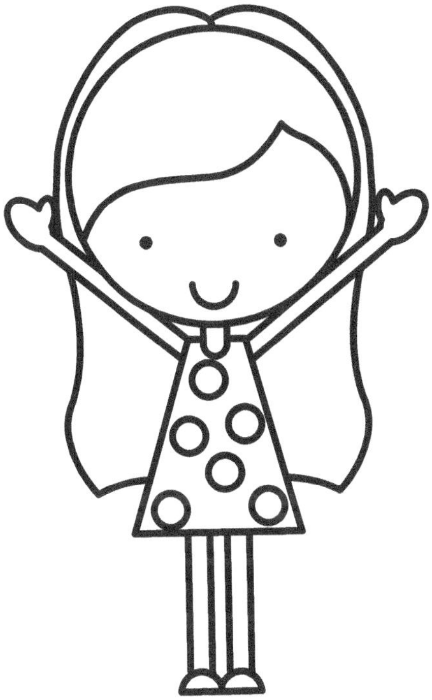

you are amazing

Never ever forget, even for a moment, how truly amazing you are!

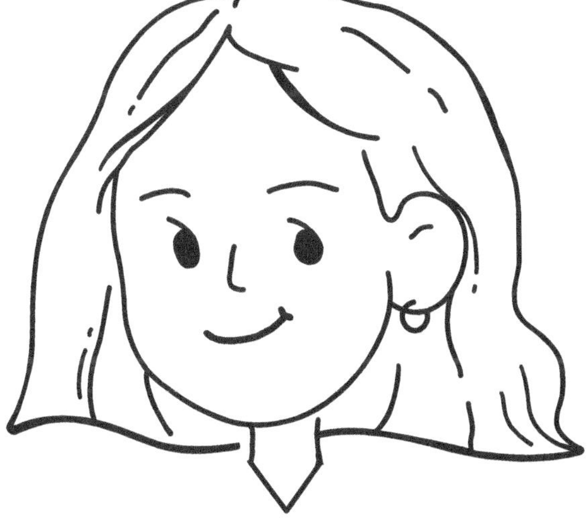

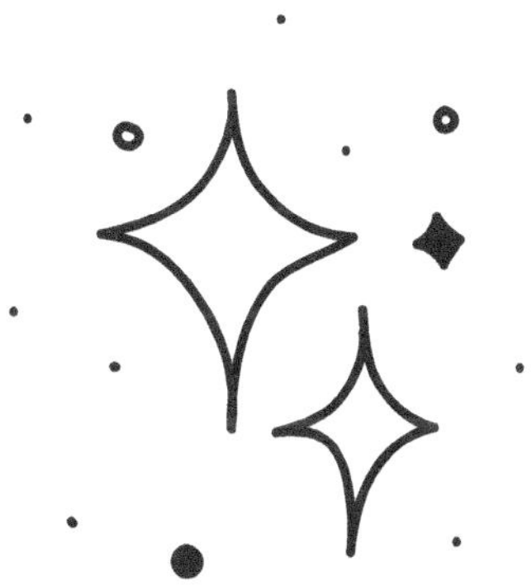

YOU ARE SO LOVED

Being deeply loved gives you strength.

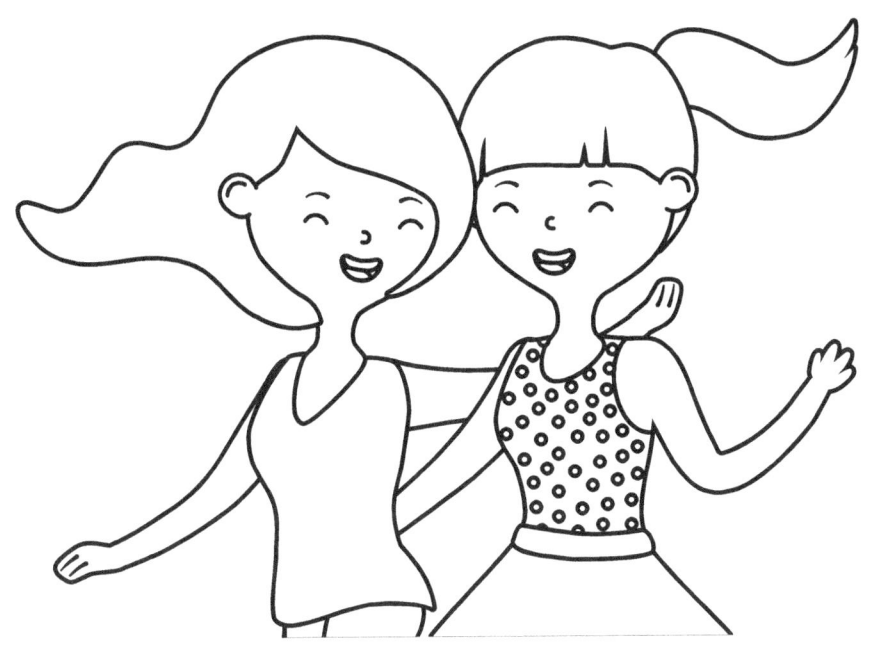

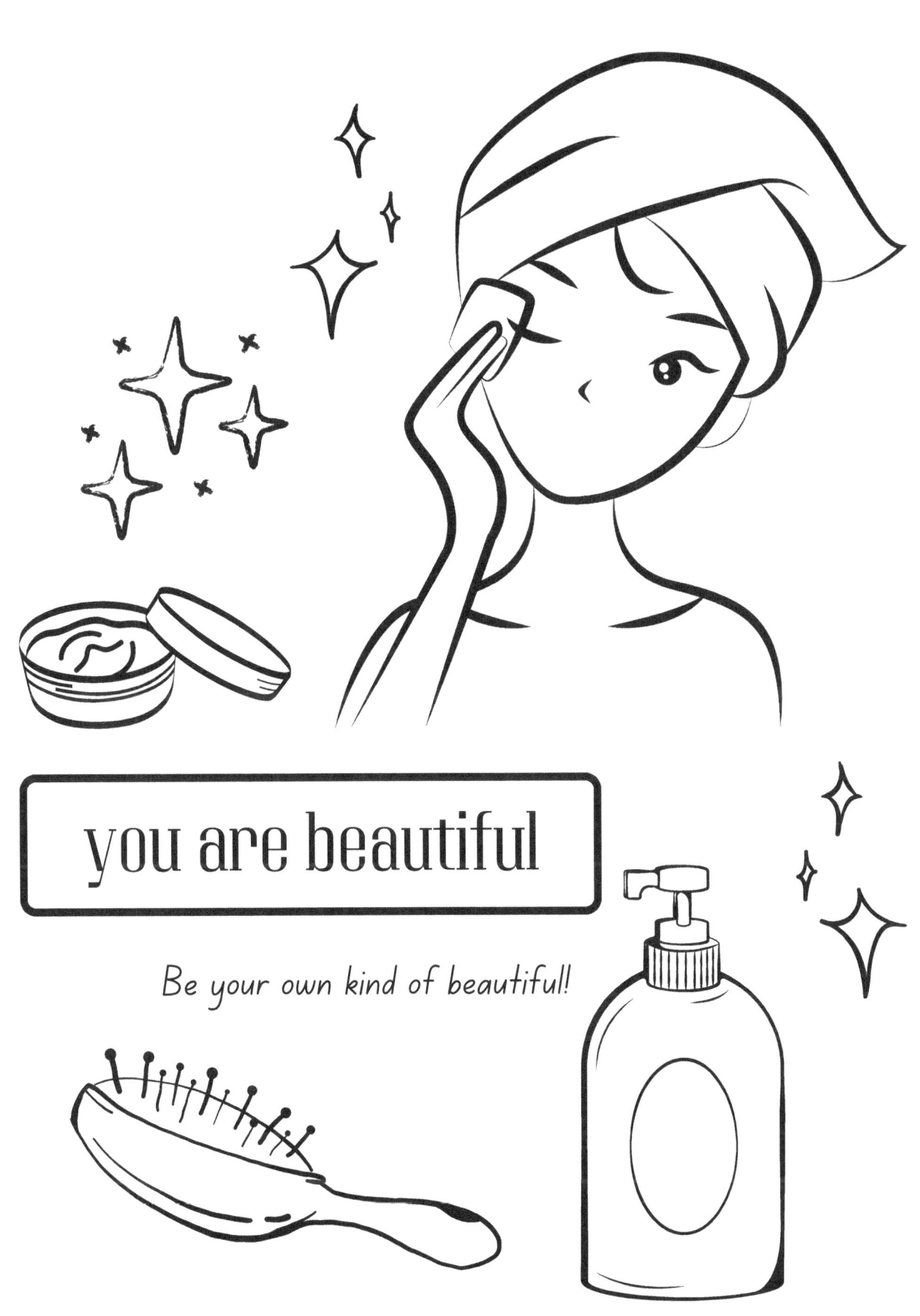

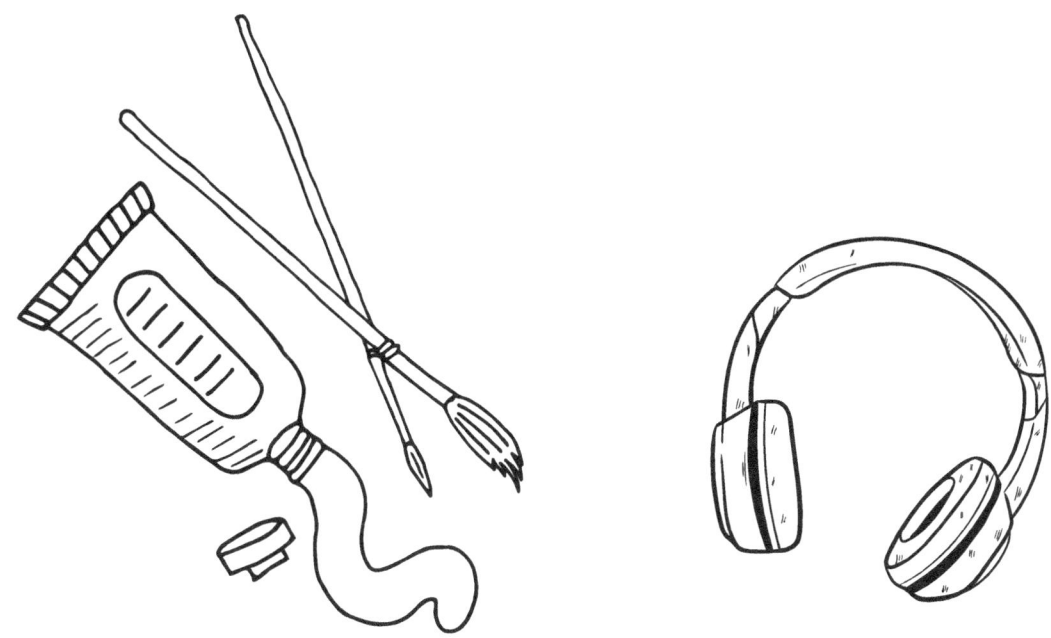

you have many talents

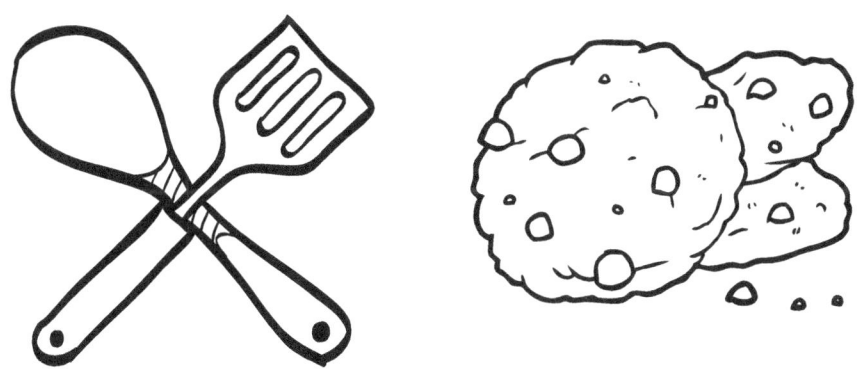

If you're young and talented, it's like you have wings.

you are worthy

You deserve every good thing!

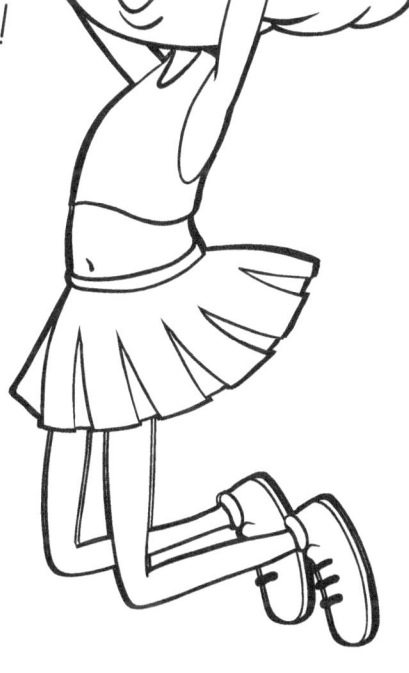

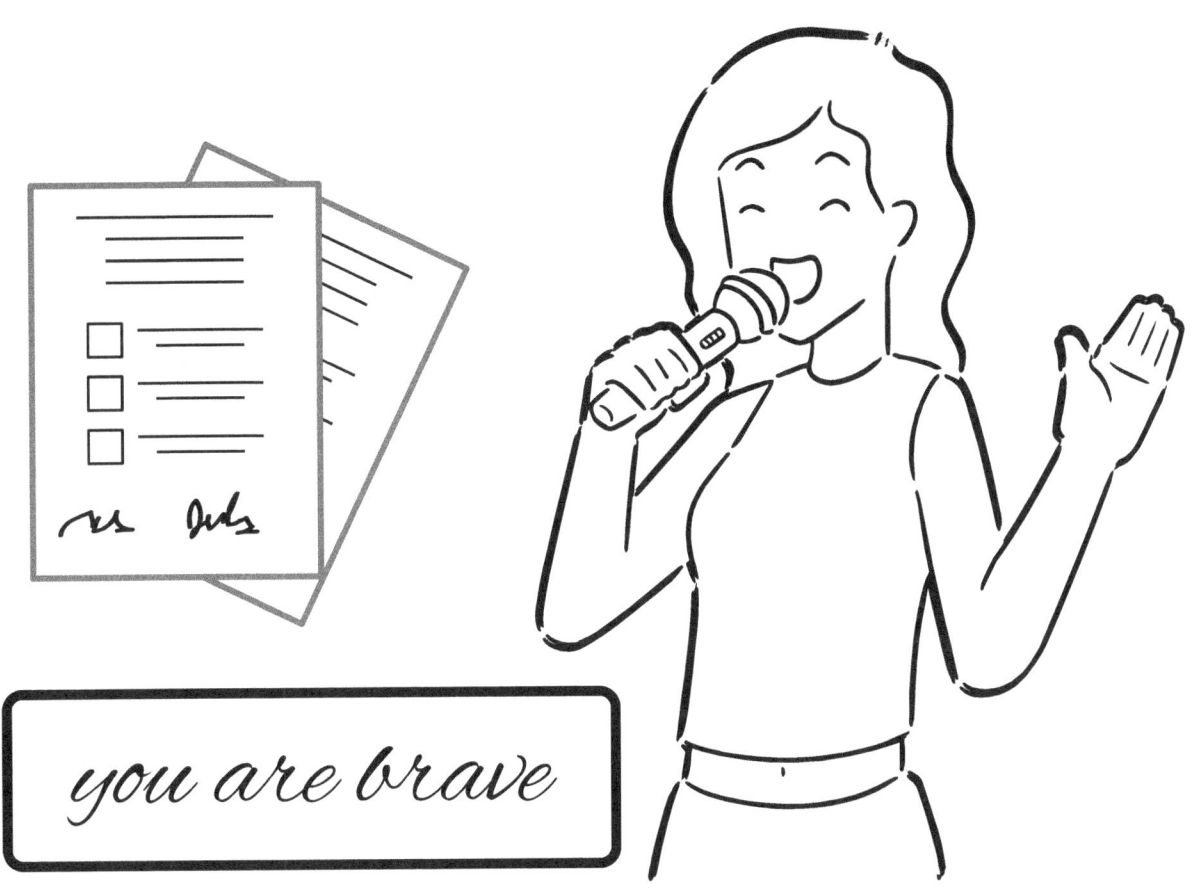

Being brave means you create the world you want to live in.

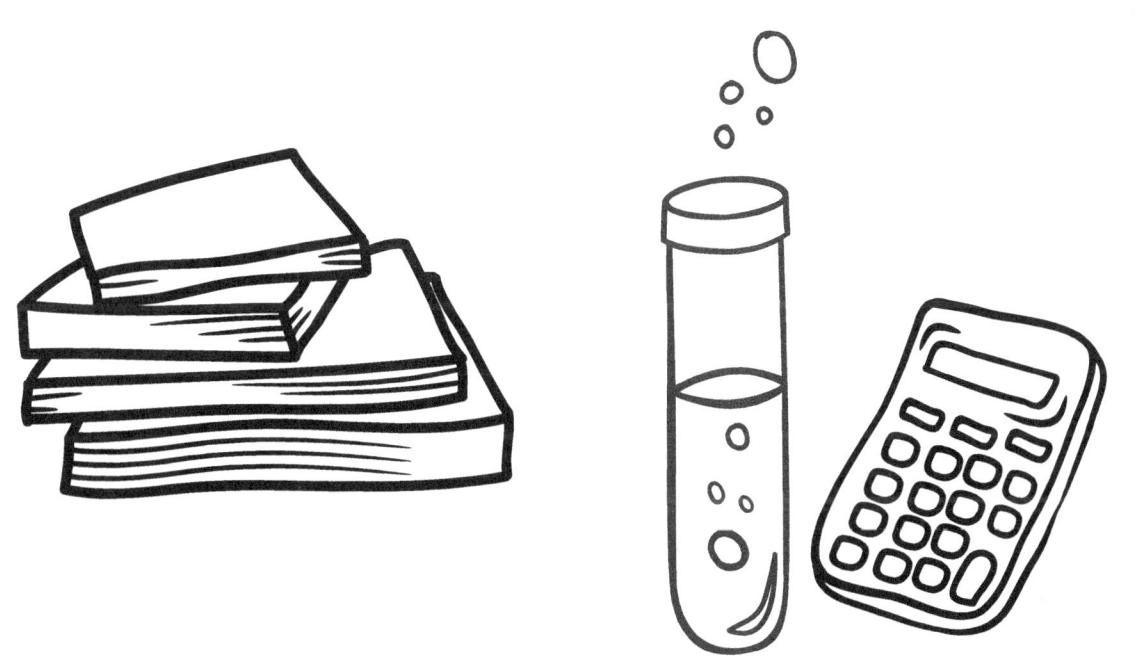

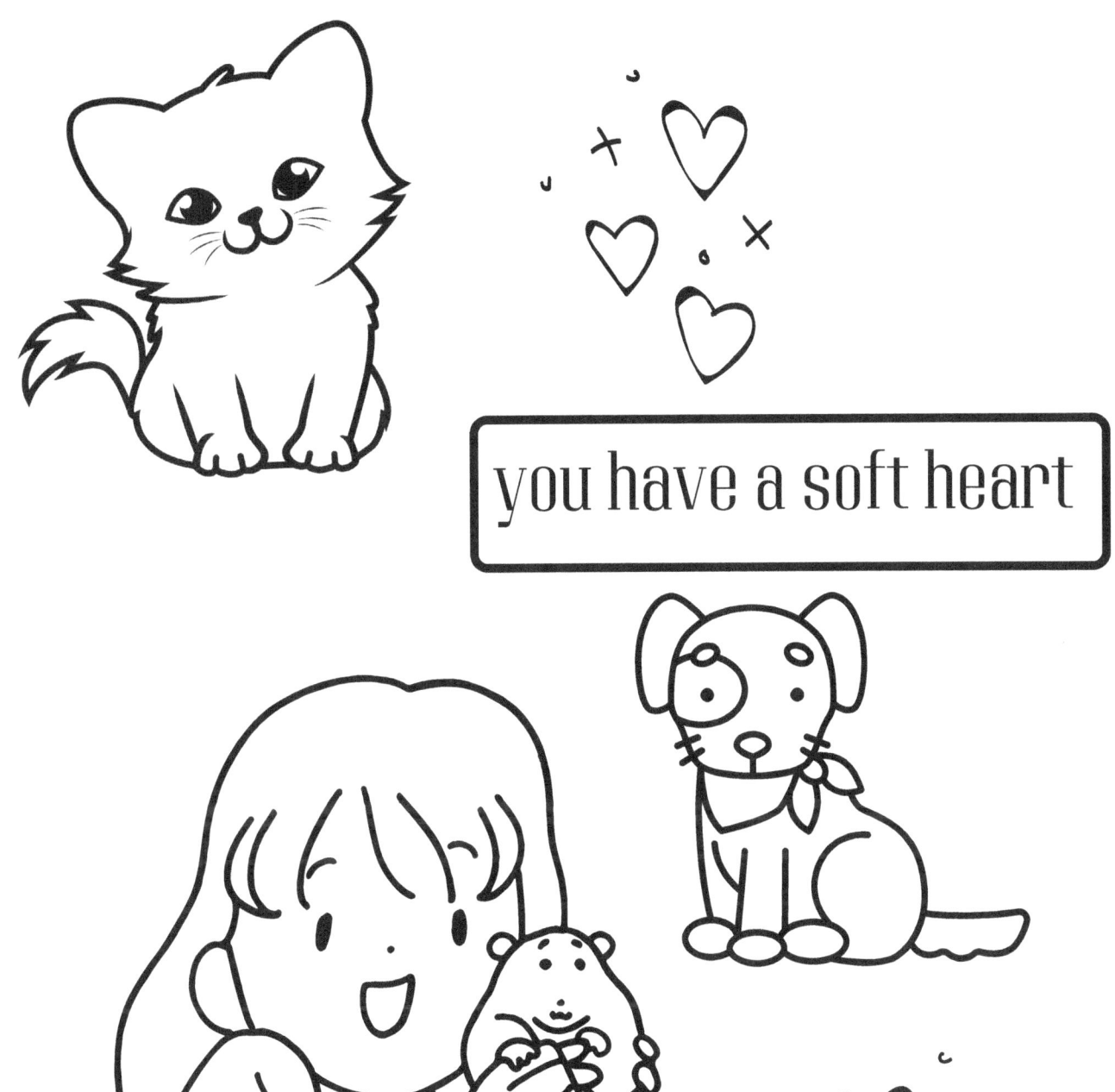

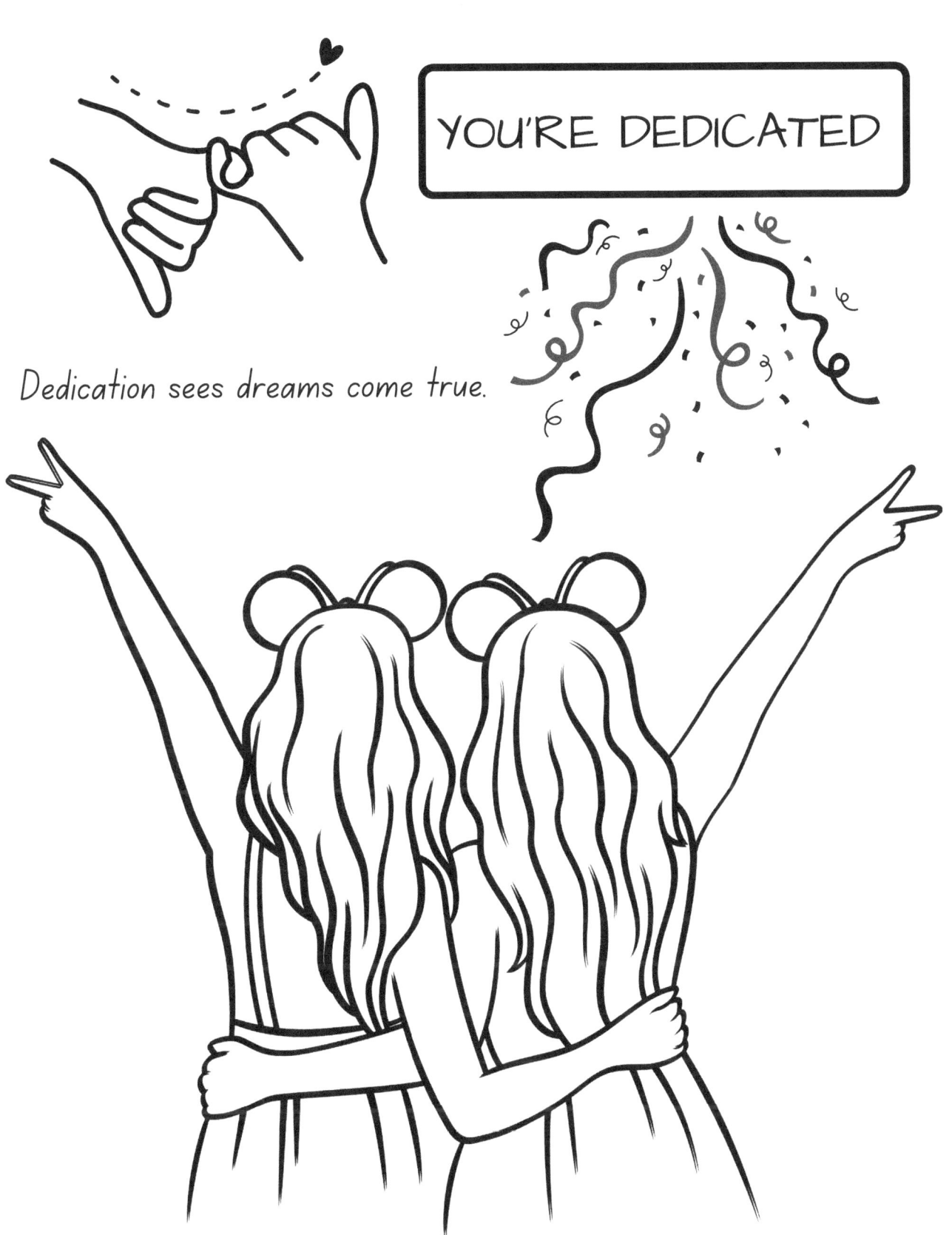

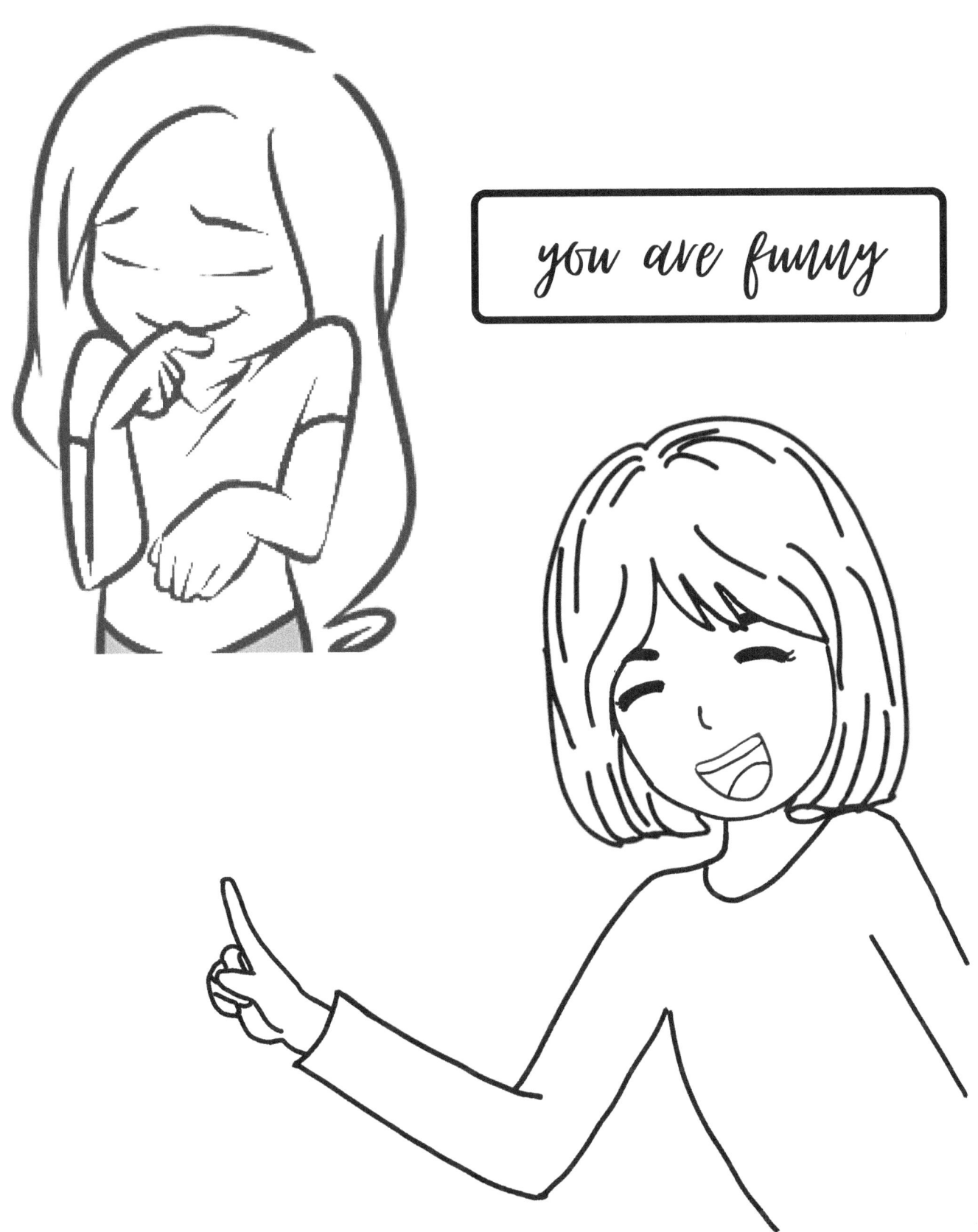

Humor is not a mood, but a way of looking at the world.

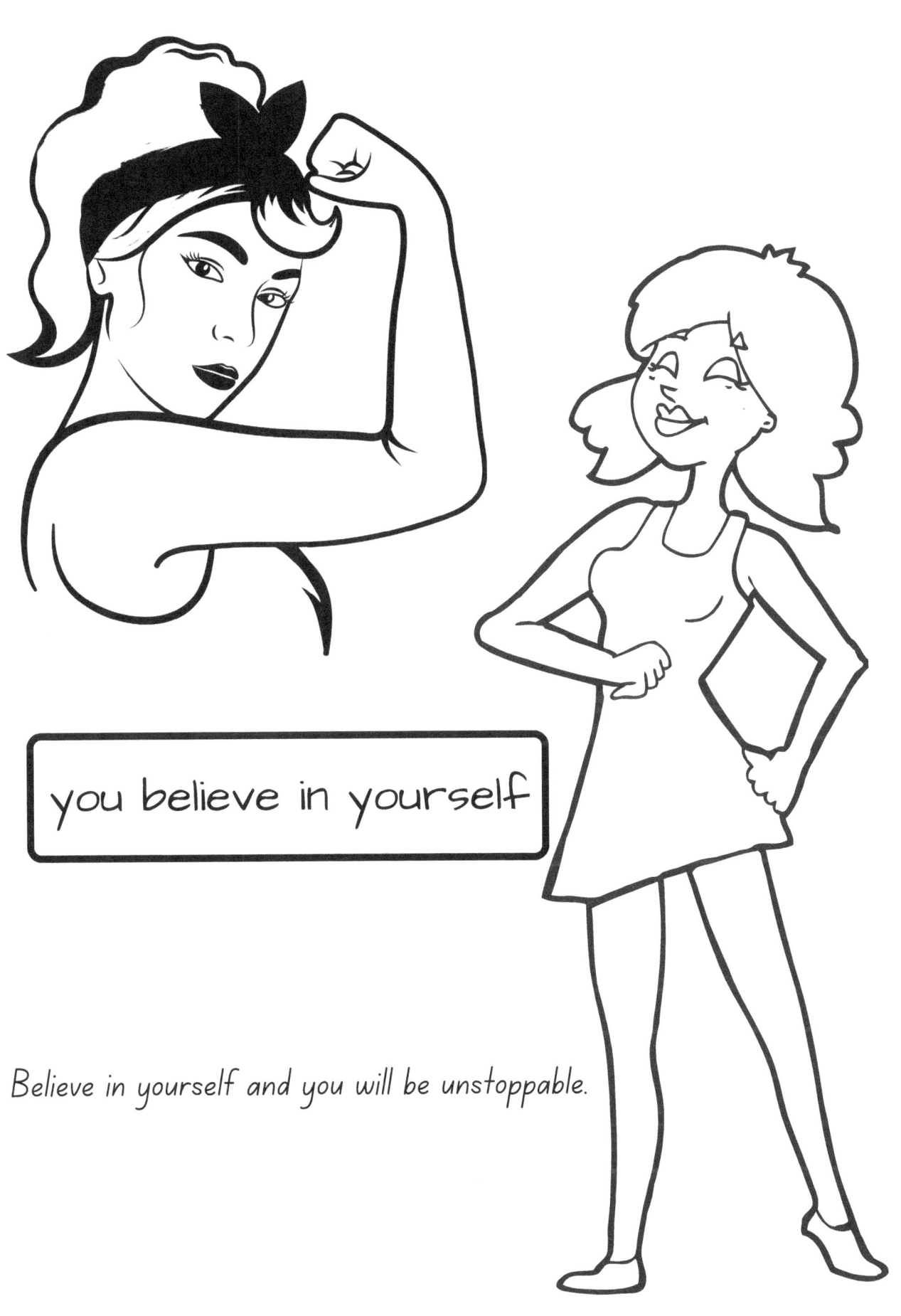

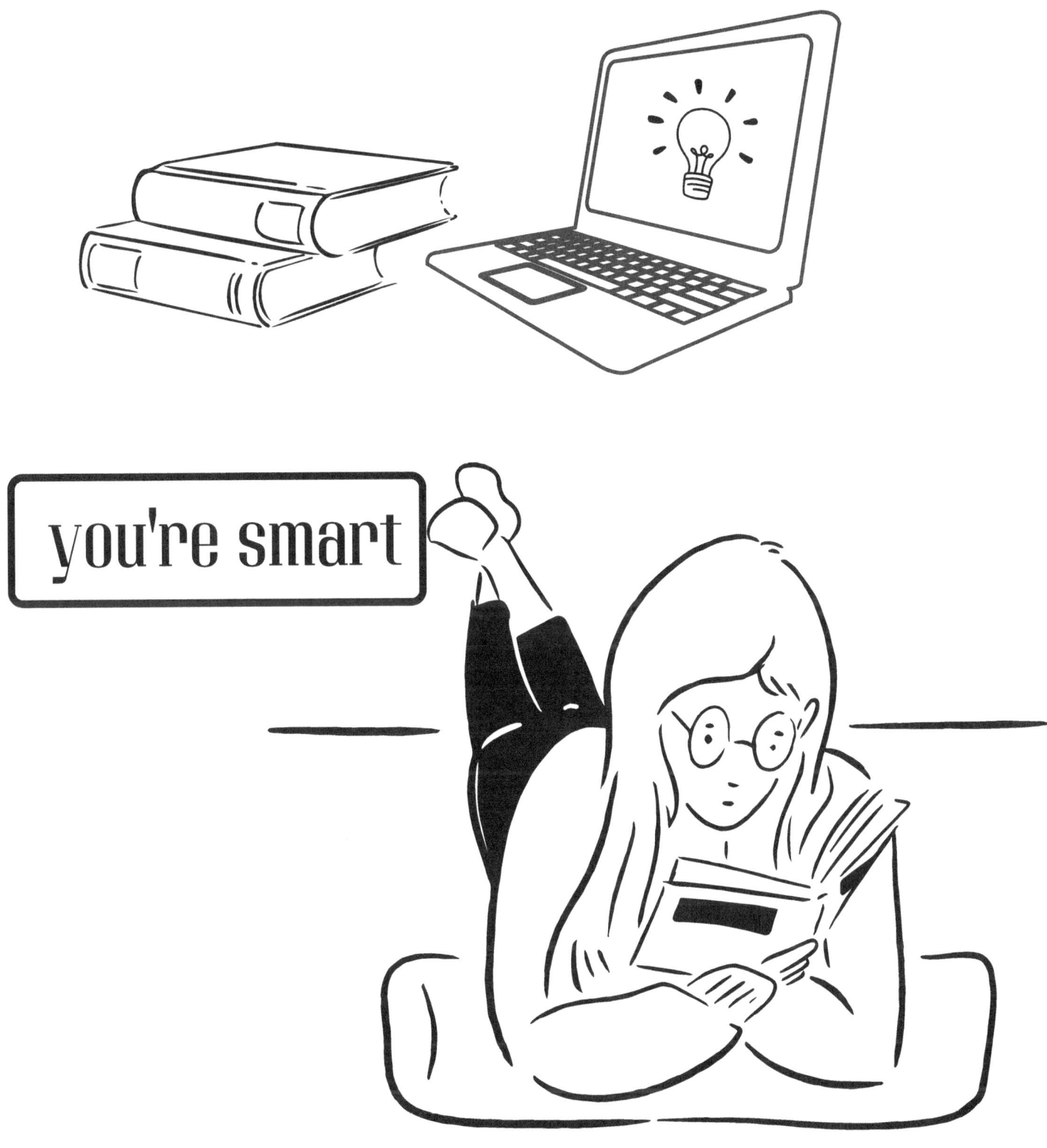

A wise person knows there is something to be learned from everyone.

YOU'RE A GOAL SETTER

Setting goals is the first step in turning the invisible into the visible.

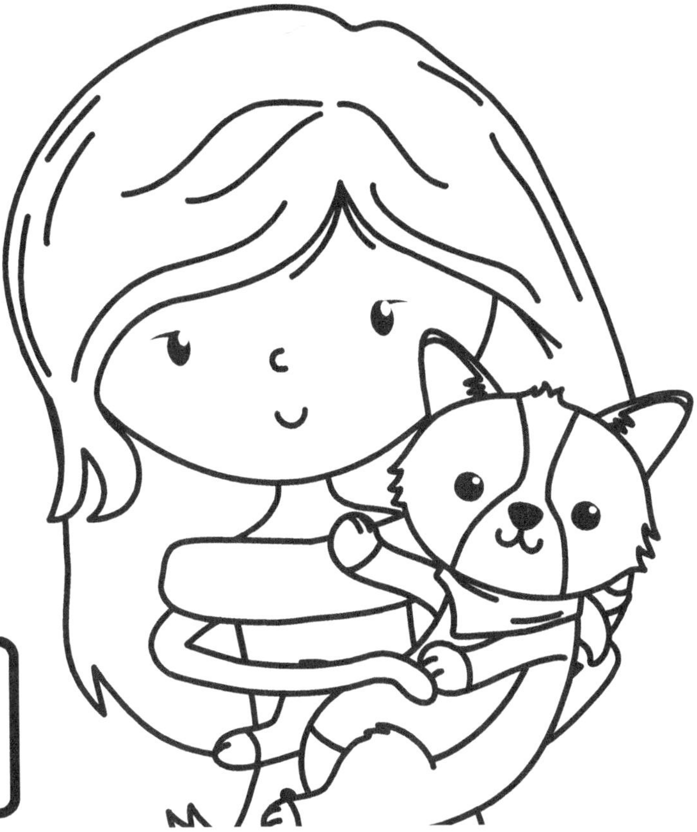

you are kind

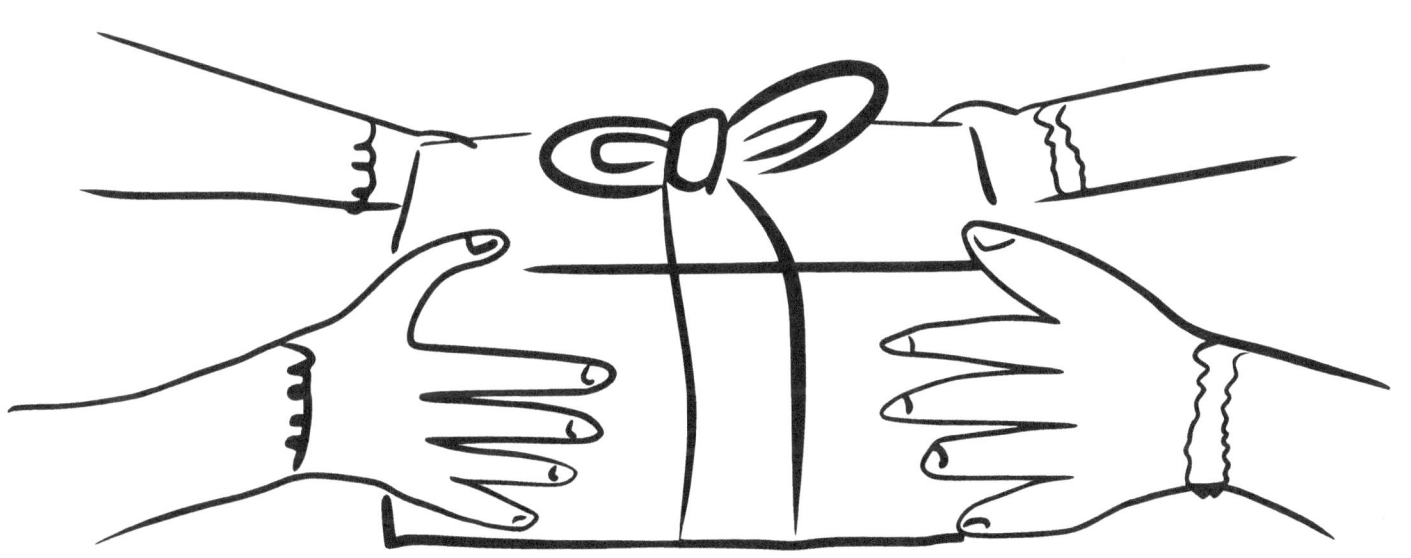

Never look down on anybody, unless you're helping them up.

you are loyal

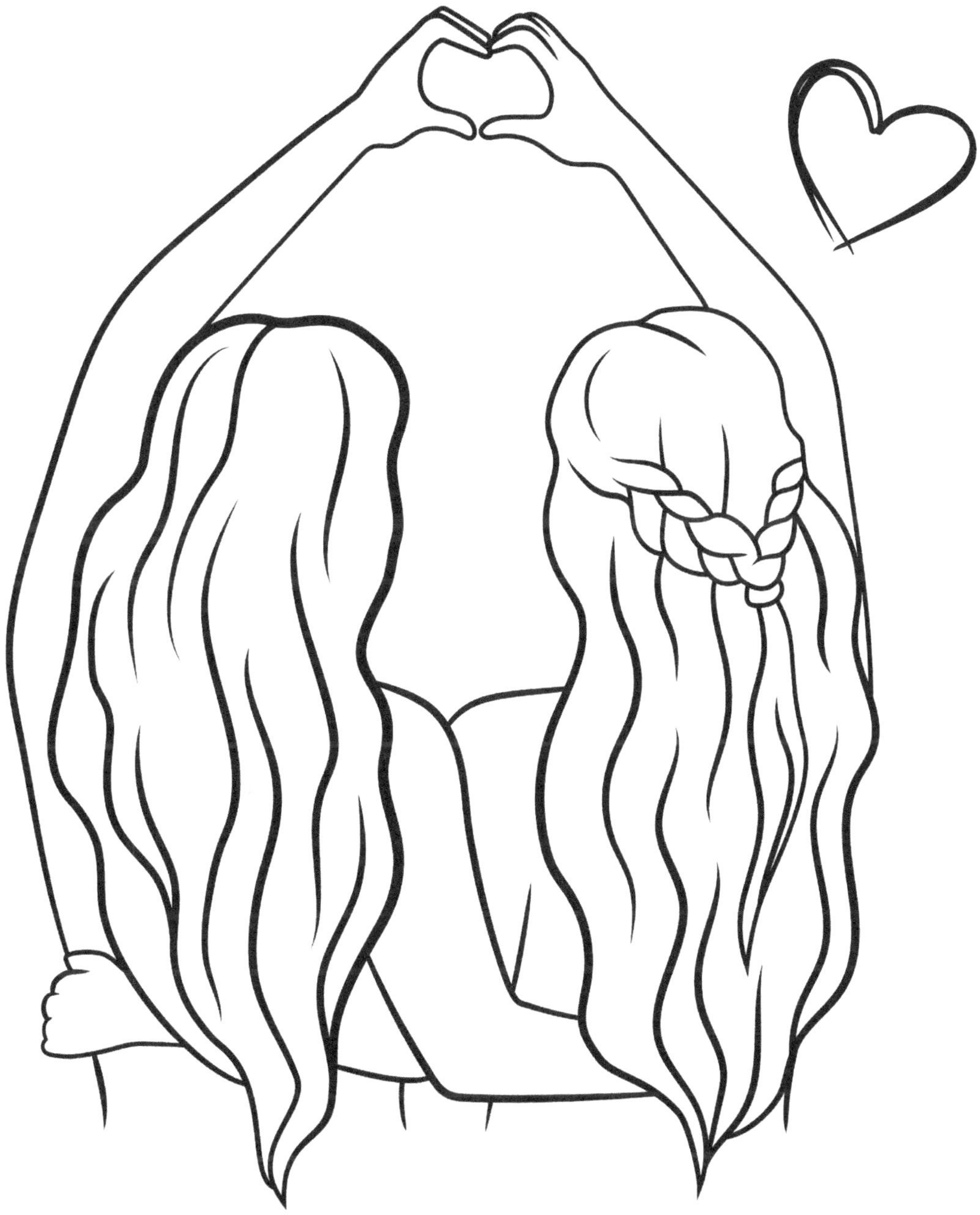

Look out for people who look out for you, loyalty is everything.

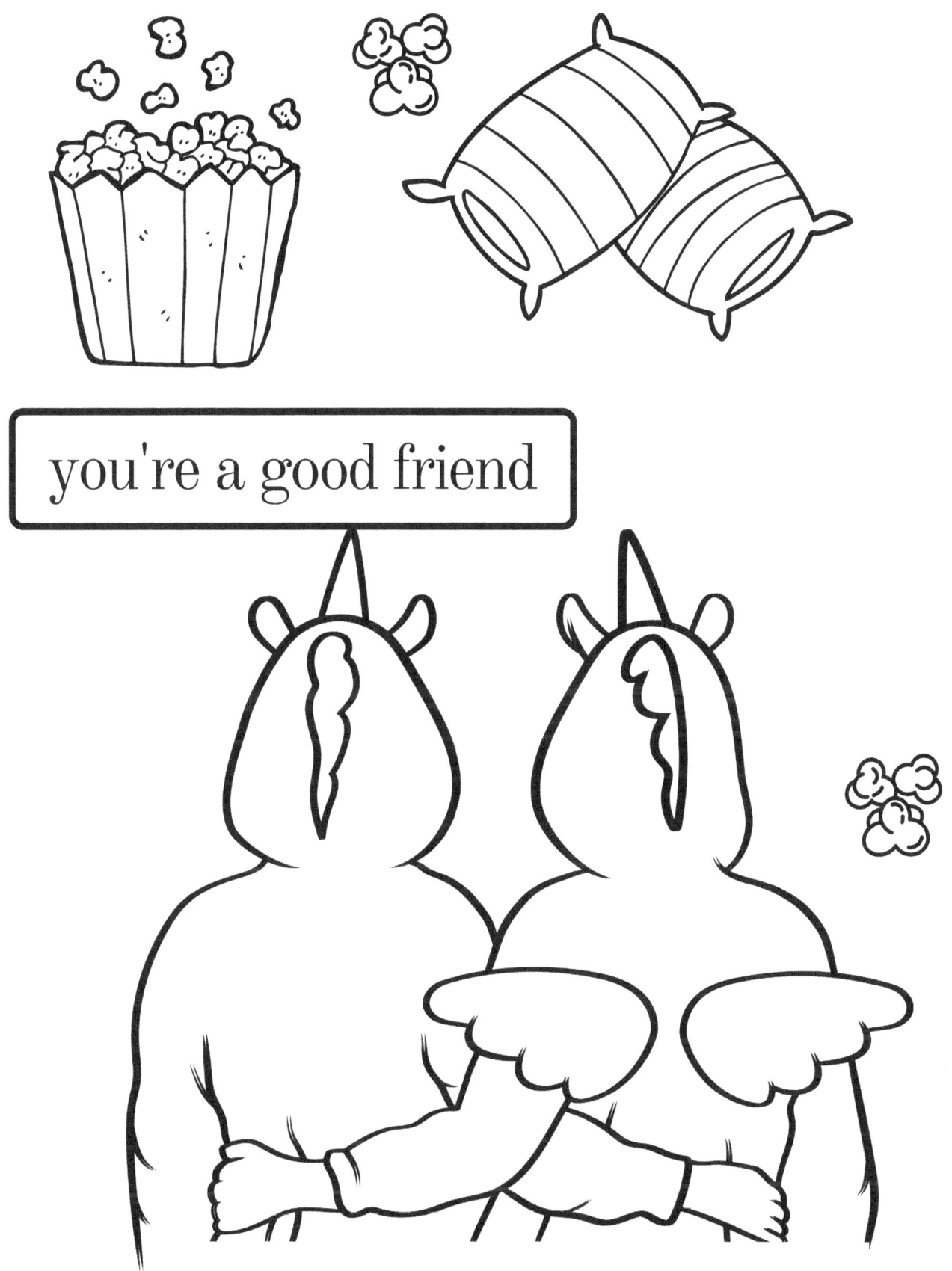

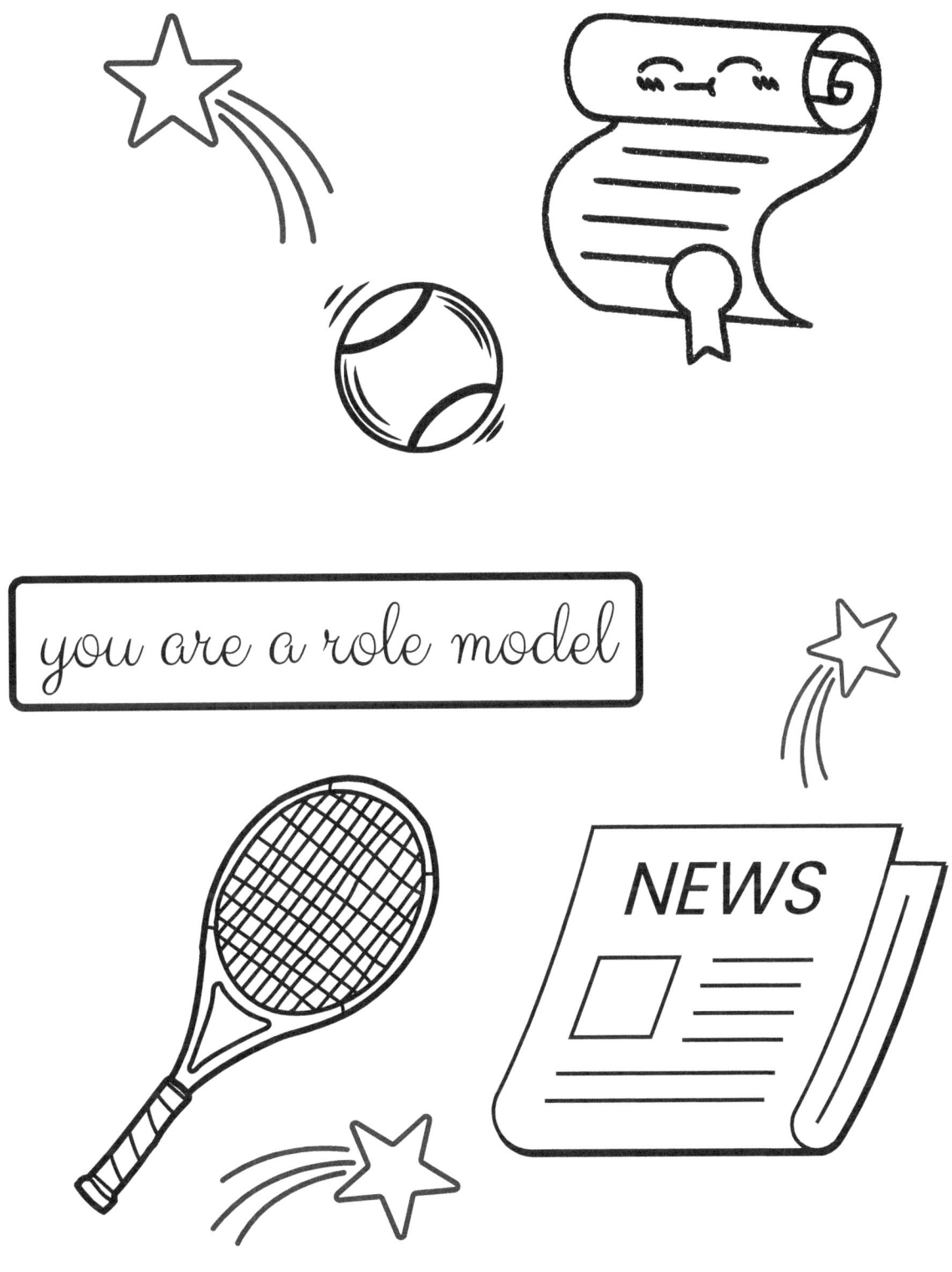

Being a role model is the most powerful form of education.

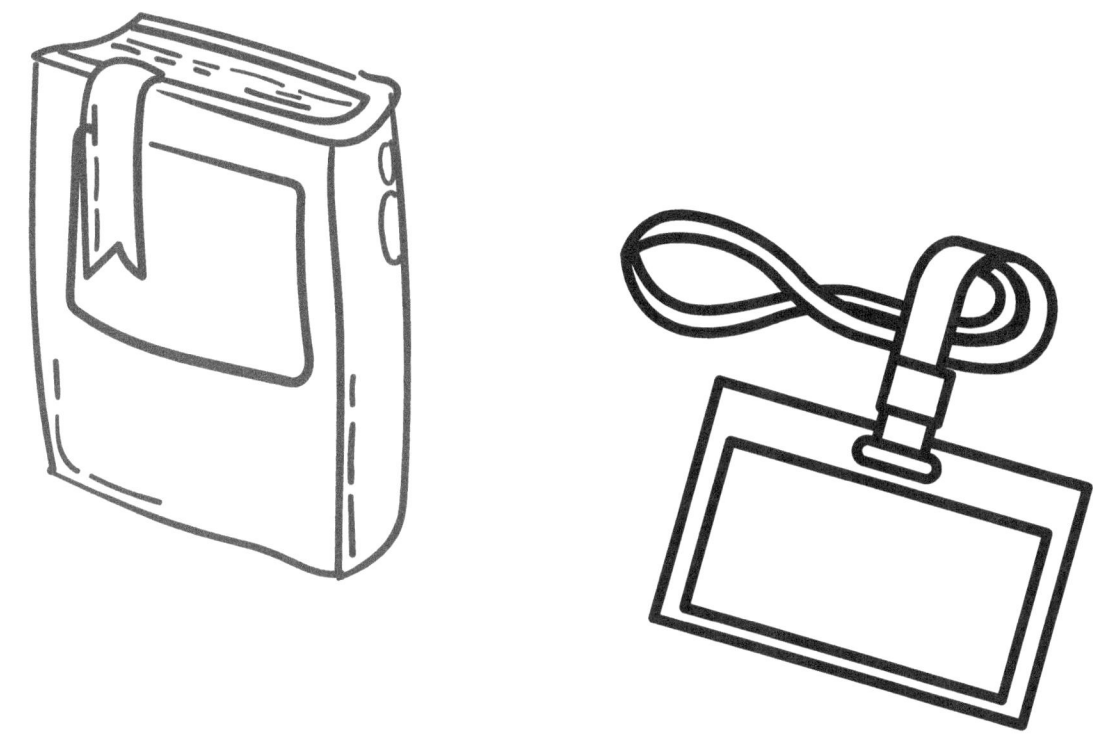

you're a hard worker

The harder you work, the more luck you have.

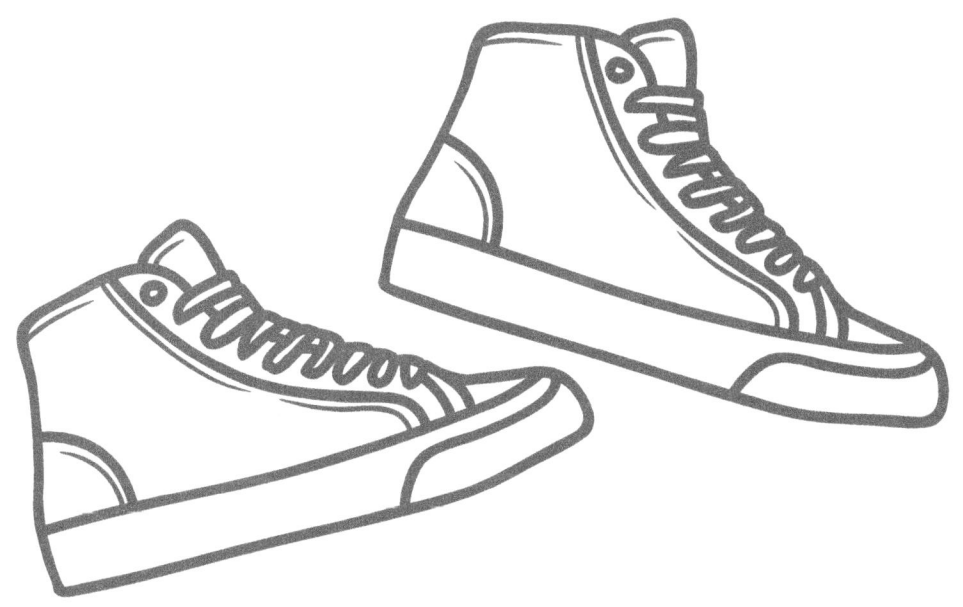

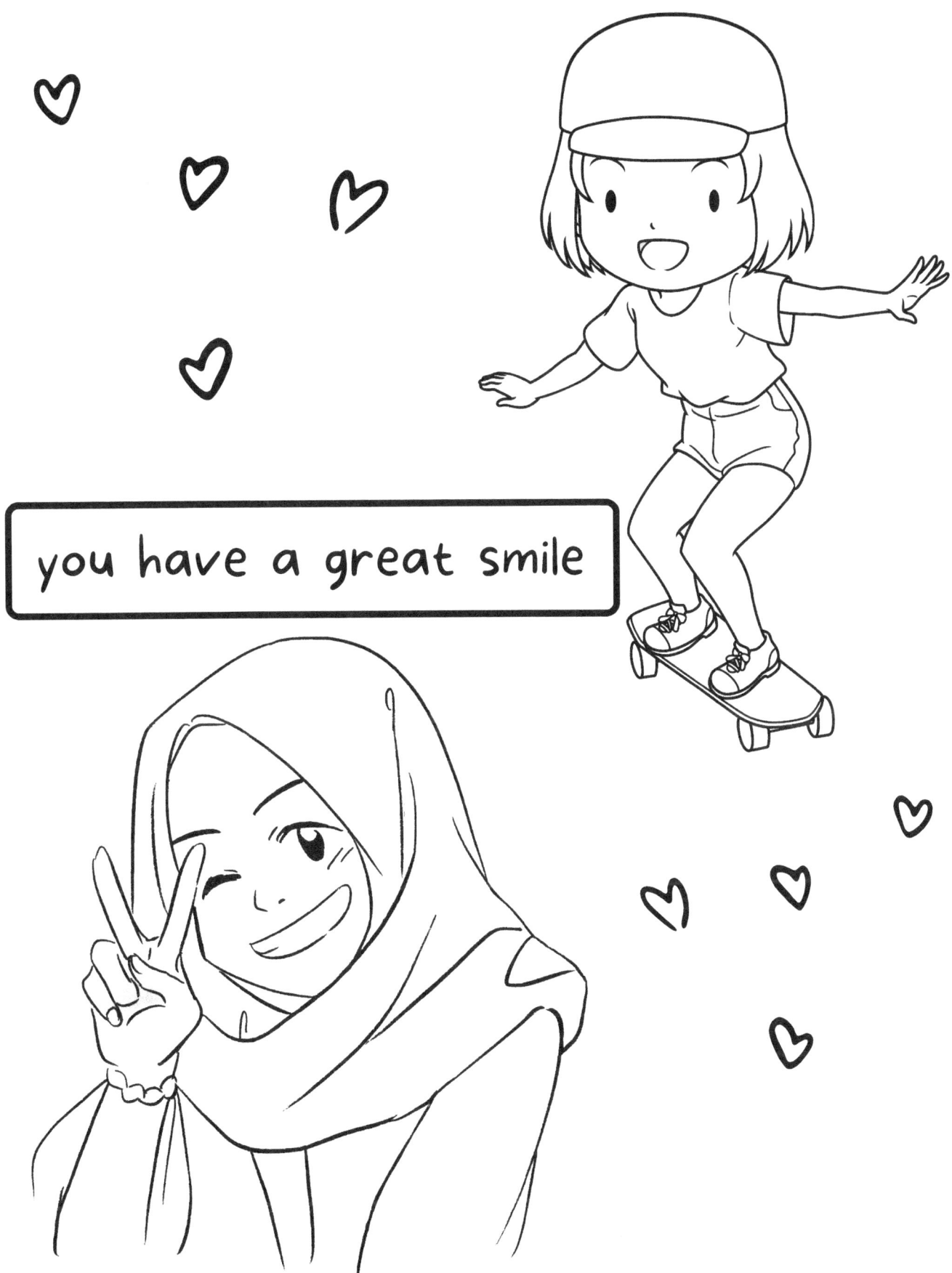

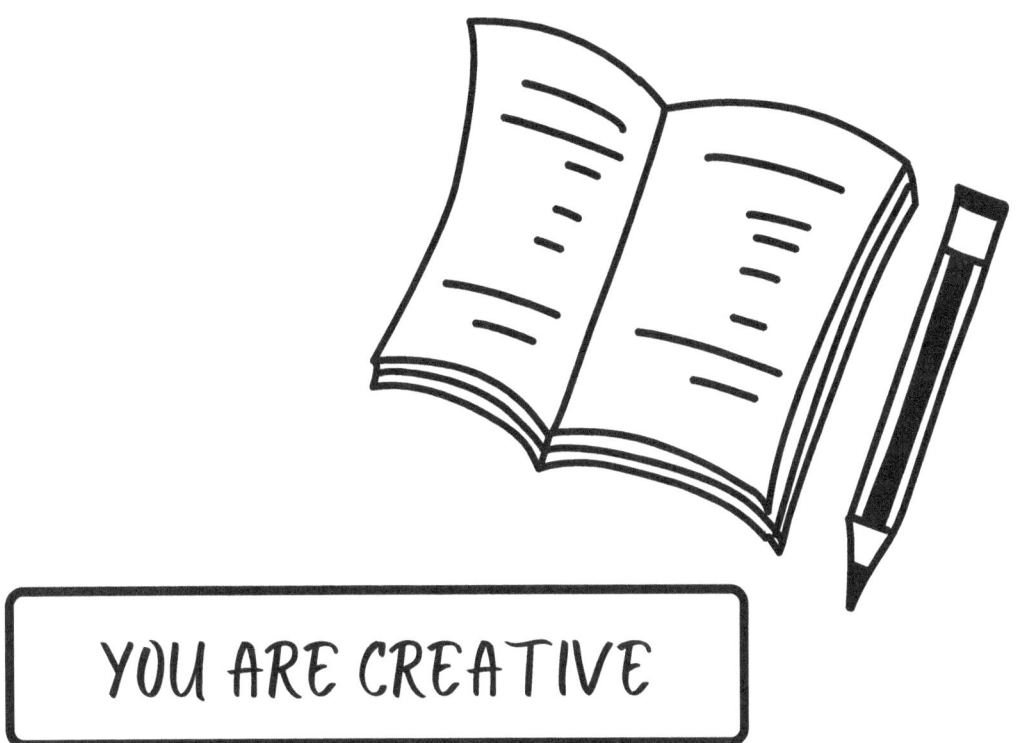

YOU ARE CREATIVE

Creativity is intellligence having fun.

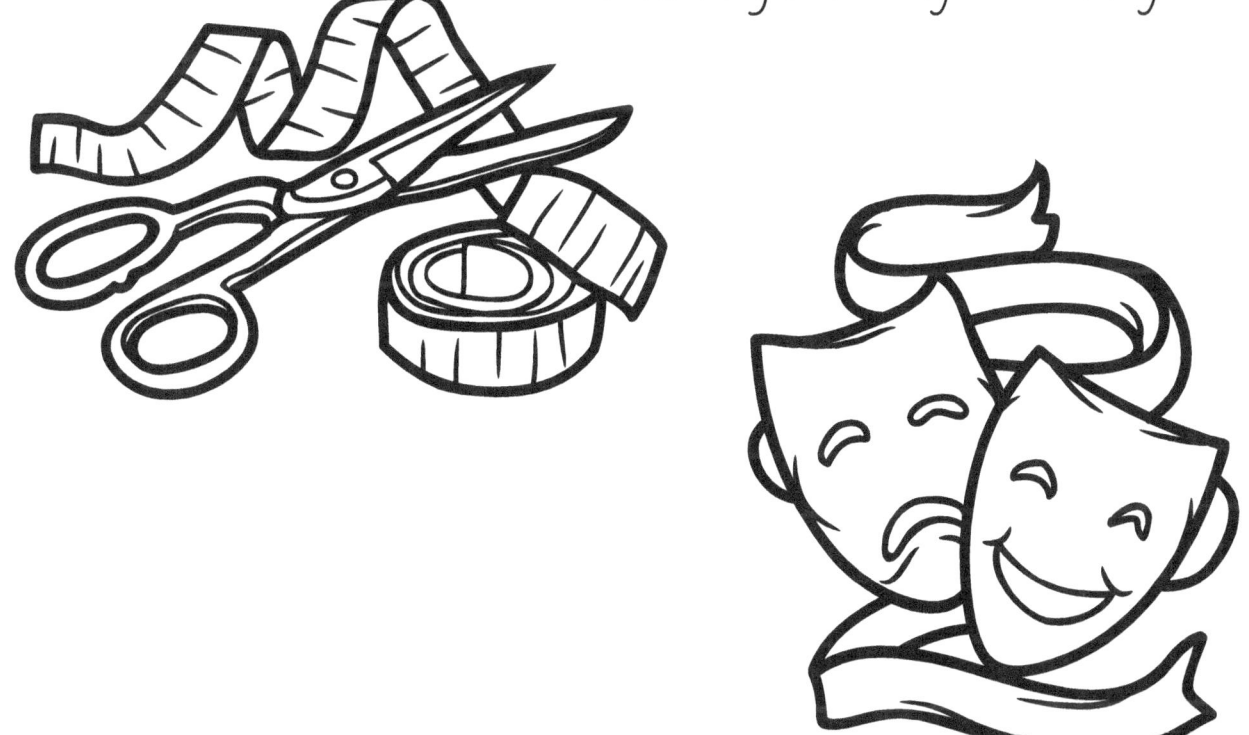

You are perfectly you!

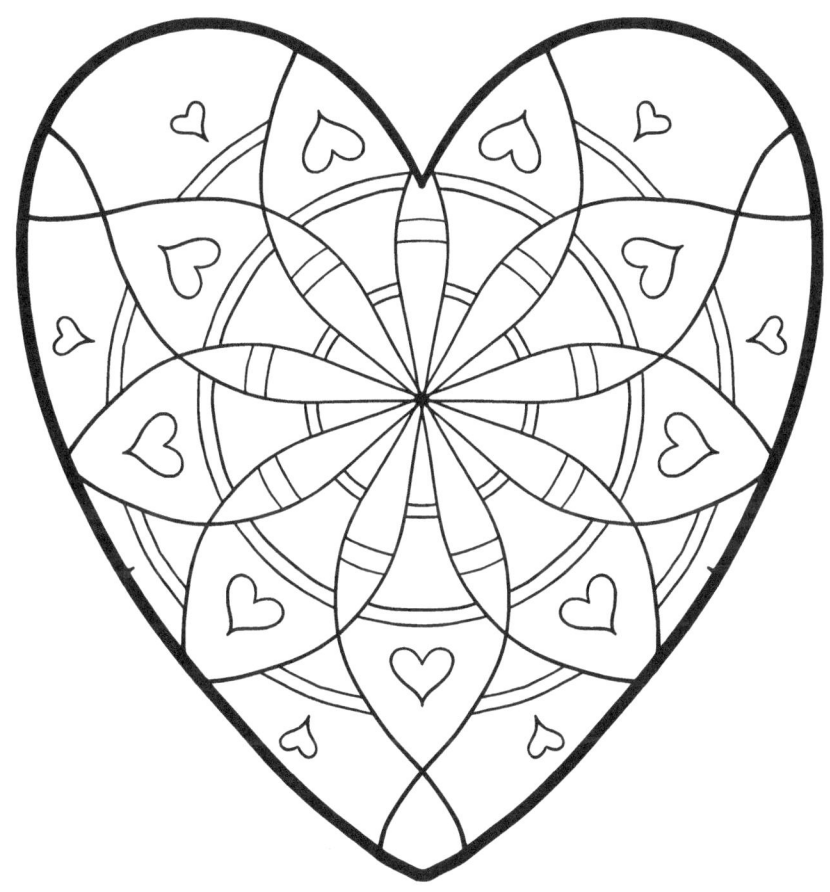

Be bold, be brave enough to be your true self!

My Dear Girl, you are amazing
YOU ARE SO LOVED   you are beautiful
you have many talents   you are worthy
you are brave   you have a soft heart
YOU'RE DEDICATED   you are funny
you believe in yourself   you're smart
YOU'RE A GOAL SETTER   you are kind
you are loyal   you're a good friend
you are a role model   you're a hard worker
you have a great smile   YOU ARE CREATIVE
you are perfectly you!

I hope you loved this book!
If you did, please leave a review
on Amazon so other girls can find it.
Thanks!

More coloring books by Ms. Josephine's Papers that you may enjoy.

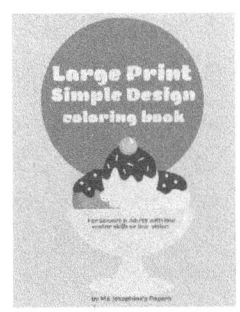 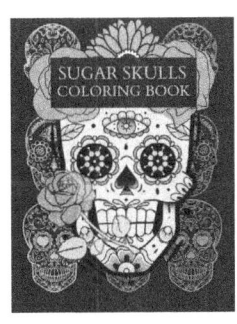 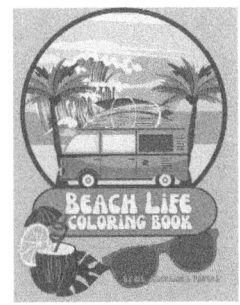 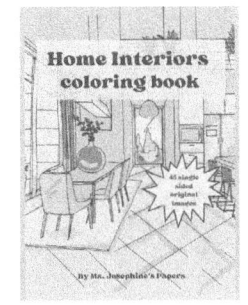 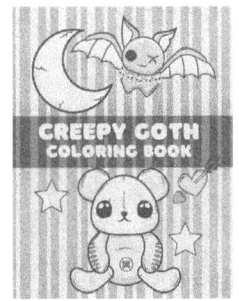

www.ingramcontent.com/pod-product-compliance
Lightning Source LLC
Chambersburg PA
CBHW081104240526
45465CB00026B/3316